Fantasy SEX

THIS IS A CARLTON BOOK

Text and design copyright © Carlton
Books Limited 2009

This edition published by
Carlton Books Limited
20 Mortimer Street
London W1T 3JW

10 9 8 7 6 5 4 3

A CIP catalogue record for
this book is available from
the British Library.

ISBN 978 1 84732 362 0

Printed in China

Senior Executive Editor:
Lisa Dyer
Managing Art Director:
Lucy Coley
Designer: Zoë Dissell
Copy Editor: Nicky Gyopari
Production: Kate Pimm

Fantasy SEX

Lisa Sweet

CARLTON
BOOKS

Contents

Introduction

You don't have to be into high-kink sex games to indulge your inner porn star. Role-playing (pretending you are somebody else) gives you a chance to indulge in some imaginary games and play at something different from your usual bedroom personality. Think of it as a way to get it on with someone new every night without cheating!

In fact, role-playing can actually tighten your love bonds. While trying on a persona different from your usual day-to-day self is mostly about giving a racy refreshment to your usual romps, it will also help to build trust between you and your partner, and deepen and enrich your relationship. After all, what could be more revealing than acting out your favourite shiver-me-timbers Captain Hook daydream? Just deciding what fantasy you want to act out, getting the equipment and planning the scene together, as a couple, can make you feel closer – not to mention turned on.

Plus, role-playing makes any sexperimentation seem more *au natural* – it's much easier to spank your lover when you are pretending to be the disciplining teacher and they are the oh-so-naughty student.

Read on for over 30 passion plots to help you both get in character. Each scene has all the info you need to heat up the action. Be prepared to leave reality on the floor – with your day clothes.

Dressing Up

Although props and costumes aren't really all that necessary for creating a sexy scene, they will make it a whole lot easier to shimmy into your chosen character. Besides, it's lots more fun to get into fancy dress than to wear your everyday clothes when role-playing. After all, this kind of pretend sex should never be a quickie.

From your knickers to your coat (and especially the shoes), dress appropriate to your role. Once you have decided who you want to be, raid your closet. Chances are, you already have lots of outfits that can double up. But if you do need to add some bits and pieces, hit up the charity shops for items like miniskirts, blouses and shirts. Discount stores are the best place to grab inexpensive, body-hugging clothes (maybe even choose a size smaller than you normally wear), lingerie, thigh-high stockings and fishnet hosiery.

If you want to go all-out or need a specific uniform, shop post-Halloween for the best bargains. Otherwise, sex-supply shops like Anne Summers (www.annsummers.com), Love Honey (www.lovehoney.co.uk), Temptations (www.temptationsdirect.co.uk) and Tabooboo (www.tabooboo.com) all have a huge selection of costumes in pretty much every theme imaginable (Elvis, anyone?). Also try fancy dress and costume supply shops like www.partydomain.co.uk. Toy stores are another good source for costumes as well as inexpensive props like handcuffs, hats, badges, fake guns and swords and other titillating trimmings.

Also, accessorize, accessorize, accessorize. Wigs, gloves, jewellery, ties, hats, glasses, wings, boots and bags not only put those oh-so-seductive finishing touches to your look — they can be used as instruments of seduction. Think of what you can do with a pair of stockings or a leather belt. Mmmm.

Keep things just this side of real by making sure that you stock up on the tools of your trade. Business people need briefcases, teachers need rulers, cops need handcuffs, doctors need stethoscopes, pilots need hats, cowboys need lassos, porn stars need big boobs (this is where that push up bra comes in handy!)... the list goes on. It's up to you how close to reality you want to get (for instance, if you are an innocent school girl, you will want to have a sweet soapy scent but if you are a firefighter, you might want to skip the ashy burnt toast aroma).

Lastly, set the stage. Most role-play fantasies can be played out without ever leaving your house – or even your bedroom, for that matter. After all, it's where your mind takes you that gives this sort of game-playing its spice. But the more props, decorations and other items you add to give your scene a realistic edge, the easier it will be to stay in role. So if you are in a harem, load the room with cushions. If it's more of a hotel atmosphere you are after, remove all personal items from the room (and stick a Bible in a drawer). But be realistic – if you have a pirate fantasy in mind, a toy scabbard slipped between the legs to part them could be highly erotic. A real scabbard, on the other hand, might result in a visit to emergency.

13

Dress-Up Mess-Ups

Don't flirt with disaster. Here's how to plot your scene so that nothing goes wrong.

If you are...
stressed out about your fantasies, let alone the thought of sharing them

Stop and breathe. Acting a scene is so perfectly normal that you've probably already done it without realizing it – talking dirty and baby talk are all types of role-playing. But if you are still unsure if you are ready for prime time play, try getting into your role in cyberspace – Second Life, Sociolotron and EverQuest are just a few games that help you explore virtual debauchery. So you can decide if getting into a scene as a client seduced by her trainer is for you without joining a gym or even investing in a pair of sneakers.

If you are...

worried that your partner will freak at your
steamy scenario suggestion, try these four tips:

1

Go slow – the first date, or five, is
probably not the time to show up
at their door dressed like one of the
Fantastic Four and expect them to let
you overpower them. Your would-be
partner won't just slam the door in
your face – they'll probably change the
locks and their name.

2

Test the waters – take your scenario from a movie with a similar theme (rent it and watch it together so it's fresh in your lover's mind). As if you are just musing out loud, casually say, "I wonder what it would be like to do it with a pilot in the cockpit" (or insert your favourite character and scene).

These 10 films have a starring role for you (see also pages 80–82 for more ideas)...

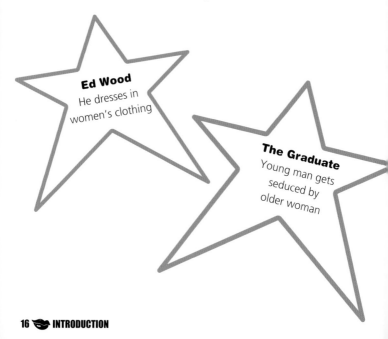

Ed Wood
He dresses in women's clothing

The Graduate
Young man gets seduced by older woman

The Hunger
Girl-on-girl vampire sex – bite me!

Street of a Thousand Pleasures
Sex-slave harems

Secretary
A feast of mind games, humiliation, bondage and beatings

The Lover

A young virgin is taught the ropes by an older suave lover

Boogie Nights

Porn star tryouts – 'nuff said

Barbarella

Sci-Fi buffs will get off on the high cult mix of zero-gravity spacesuits and attempted murder by orgasm

Crimes of Passion
She is a fashion designer by day and a kinky prostitute by night (as if she could be anything else)

Dangerous Liaisons
Sexy seduction set again the lush costume-drama decadence of 18th-century France

And three all-in-ones:

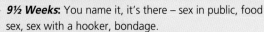 ***9½ Weeks:*** You name it, it's there – sex in public, food sex, sex with a hooker, bondage.

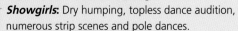 ***Showgirls:*** Dry humping, topless dance audition, numerous strip scenes and pole dances.

⭐ ***Caligula:*** Manages to pack in rape, incest, bestiality, necrophilia and sado-masochism – all while wearing togas.

3

Flattery will get you anywhere. Start with something positive and ego boosting, like "I think you are really sexy", quickly follow up with "I've been having this fantasy lately. How would you feel about trying it?" Never ever mention boredom – unless you are in the mood for a bottom bashing!

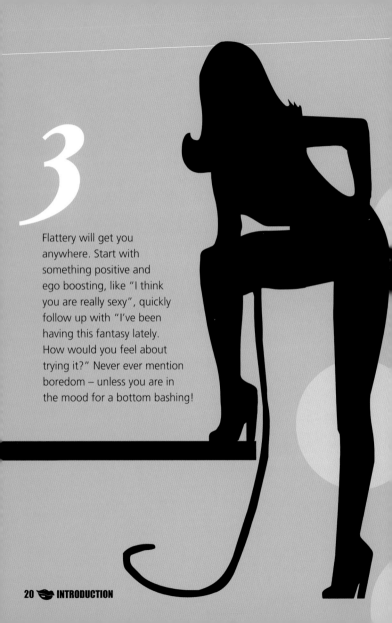

4

Casually mention that science has shown sharing your fantasies is a sign of intelligence. Seems those a few fries short of a Happy Meal have low impulse control – in other words, if they think it, they tend to do it. Brighter people, on the other hand, will think, weigh up the risks (of actually going out and seducing a stranger, for example) and fantasize instead.

If you are...
having opening night jitters

Role-playing is not about keeping your eye on the Oscar.
It would probably be a huge freakout if you or your lover
became really serious about mastering the role of rapist
or down-and-out stripper. The main thing is to have fun –
not worry about your lines or whether your costume is
100 per cent authentic.

That said, these two rules will keep you in the groove:

Build up the suspense: Don't just dive in and start acting
out the fantasy one night without any prep. Send each
other messages throughout the day when you're both
at work and actually create a story that leads to you
eventually hooking up. This could go on for a day, a week
or as long as you want. Anticipation is half the fun.

Put some effort into it: If she's playing some sort of seductress,
the whole thing gets a bit ruined if she's wearing her flannel
bunny pajamas and her hair is in bunches. And, unless he's
playing a cowboy or James Dean, wearing torn blue jeans and
T-shirt isn't going to cut it either. Remember, part of the fantasy is
that you're supposed to be different people. Look the part as well
as act the part. Buy some lingerie and a wig or fake moustache
(see pages 10–12 and 127 for resources). If you can afford it,
spend the night at a hotel. If you can't, rearrange your bedroom
so it looks like a completely different room. Do anything you can
(and you can afford to do) to make the actual event more realistic.

If you are...
having a disaster

You shimmied into the rubber catsuit and now
the zipper is stuck. This is the difference between
laying out a few quid for your costume and props
and making an investment. Synthetic roadkill wigs shed,
faux PVC makes you sweat, and cheap handcuffs get
jammed. The main thing is not to panic or get angry. Try
to work the mishap into the scene. If you can't, laugh it
off – after all, that's what this is all about. You're doing
this because you want to have fun together; you're
not in some Shakespearean play. If one of you ends up
giggling at some point, laugh with them; then, if you
can regain your composure, continue. If not, there's
always tomorrow.

If you are...
so nervous you are rushing

Pace yourselves. Take babysteps. Maybe you don't dress like a pilot and flight attendant the first time, but you talk the talk. Sometimes, all you need is a new line. You'd be surprised how far "you've been a bad baby" can go when said in the right context. Try it in public even – when your partner can't do anything about it. Suddenly, the nearest wardrobe or coat closet looks highly appealing.

If you are...
not sure what to do next

Know your character. Most of the shyness and
nervousness that comes with dressing up as
someone else and playing a role is from a
lack of preparation. It's hard to leap into
action if you've never thought about how
a French maid might sound and what
she might want to do with those feather
dusters. Once you are comfortable with
the direction you are going in, you can
get more detailed and start thinking
about the location, the time of day,
who else is around, what's going
to happen (a mind-melting orgasm,
hopefully, but how – what's the story
and where's it going?). Erotic role-play is just
like acting with a specific beginning, middle and
end. The more detail you can add to the fantasy
the more alive it becomes. Sure it requires some
effort, but is that too much to ask for an endless
string of wild nights?

Dress Codes

Set up some basic ground rules and boundaries to make sure everyone is working with the same script:

✳ No laughing or eye rolling at your partner for something they say or do. At the end of the day (and play), you need to feel good about the person you are with after the fancy dress and fake moustaches come off.

✳ Anyone can stop a scene at any time. The point of role-playing is to have fun (oh, yeah – and a mind-blowing romp).

✳ Work out a sign or word that you can use to check in with each other (after all, if you are playing a rape scene, screaming, "Stop" might come off as part of the play).

SETTING THE SCENE

Some scenes can never be lived out – especially those that go against the law of physics, nature or your local laws. But with a little effort and a bit more imagination, you can turn your fantasies into orgasmic reality.

The way to use the scenarios that follow – and the most pleasurable method for fantasy role-playing in general – is to start slowly, with simple scenes such as those scripted out in the **Getting It On Game for Newbies** sections. A big theatrical performance can make the sex too complicated and you or partner freaked. Once you have a few performances under your belt, you can start working the dialogue in **Getting It On Game for Experienced Scenesters**. Only pros should be playing the **Getting It On Game for Hardcore Role-Players**.

Don't break a leg!

Chapter One

Costume Dramas

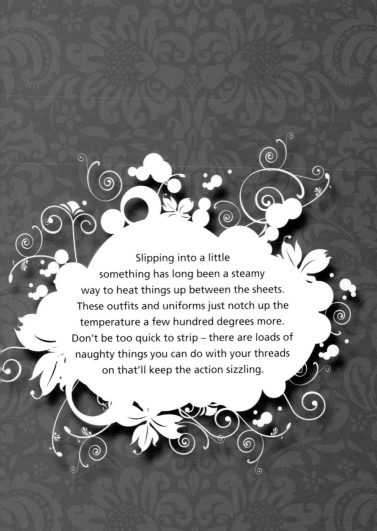

Slipping into a little
something has long been a steamy
way to heat things up between the sheets.
These outfits and uniforms just notch up the
temperature a few hundred degrees more.
Don't be too quick to strip – there are loads of
naughty things you can do with your threads
on that'll keep the action sizzling.

SCENE 1 *Prepare for Take-Off*

Basic Plot

There's a reason it is called a cockpit! You'll join the mile-high club when she dresses up as a sex-starved stewardess and he is the pleasure-seeking pilot.

Getting It On Game for Newbies

Get ready for take-off by using a room in your home as the cockpit. Set up two padded chairs side by side in front of a window. He pretends to fly the plane and calls the stewardess to the cockpit, telling her that they will be experiencing turbulence. He then proceeds to tell her – explicitly – how to put his gear in a holding pattern.

Getting It On Game for Experienced Scenesters

Start with some in-flight entertainment. As the pilot is getting ready for take-off, she uses her hand or a vibrator to bring herself to cruising altitude.

Getting It On Game for Hardcore Role-Players

Propel the scene along with some appropriate language. He asks her to come into the cockpit. She replies that she gets wet just hearing the word, "cockpit" because she loves "cock" and begs him to say it again and again. He offers to show her his instrument panel and pulls out his "equipment", saying he has put the plane on autopilot and so they have time to do whatever they want.

Dress It Up

For Him:
* Pilot Hat
* White short-sleeved shirt
  (add stripes to sleeves)
* Dark trousers
* Tie
* Airline wings badge

For Her:
* Mini-skirt and tight shirt in the same
  colour (preferably turquoise or pink)
* Wedge hat
* Scarf
* White go-go boots
* White gloves
* Airline wings brooch
* Small vibrator

XXX Rating
Use the scarf
or tie as a soft
restraint.

Make It Real

Bring along a carry-on suitcase packed with travel accessories to make sure you have a smooth flight – miniature bottles of alcohol, small packets of snacks for eating off each other, a travel pillow and blanket, and hot steamy towels to clean up.

SCENE 2

Angels & Demons

Basic Plot

He's a horny devil and she's an angel with an over-the-top innocent attitude – until he makes her his disciple!

Getting It On Game for Newbies

Plunge the room into total darkness. She lies in bed as if asleep. He suddenly appears wearing nothing more than a tail and horns and a red silk cape, brandishing a pitchfork and ready to ravish her purity.

Getting It On Game for Experienced Scenesters

He jumps into bed and makes a grab for her. But just as he touches her, she runs away from him and hides. A hot and heavy game of hide-'n'-seek follows.

Getting It On Game for Hardcore Role-Players

Virtue always triumphs over sin so she throws on the lights and takes charge, giving him a series of ultra good sexy deeds to do (to her) in order for him to find redemption – not to mention satisfaction!

Dress It Up

For Him:

* Red tail
* Red horns
* Red silk cape
* Pitchfork

For Her:

* Ultra-short floaty white dress
* Wings
* Halo
* Silver glitter
* White fishnet stockings
* Silver glitter heels
* Wand

XXX Rating

Instead of a pitchfork, he can brandish a red dildo and use it as his devil's little helper.

Make It Real

He should use plenty of "bleeped" language. The more he graphically describes what he's going to do to her, the more she flinches, as if her oh-so-angelic innocence is being tarnished.

SCENE 3 WILD, WILD, WILD WEST

Basic Plot

Childhood games of cowboys and Indians get hot and heavy when they're played grown-up style.

Getting It On Game for Newbies

If you don't have nosey neighbours, start your game outside. Otherwise, you can stalk each other in your house. Stealth and silence are all-important as she sneaks up on him and takes him captive by surprise. Once she has him prisoner, he begs for a peace powwow during which he gives her everything she wants.

Getting It On Game for Experienced Scenesters

She refuses, saying he is in her power. She undresses him and ties him up, just tight enough to that he cannot escape. Should she scalp him, burn him at the stake or abandon him to fry under the hot sun? Instead, she removes a feather from her headdress and tickle tortures him. Ever so slowly she drags the feather across his naked body until he screams for mercy.

Getting It On Game for Hardcore Role-Players

He overpowers her and, using his lasso, binds them both together into a tight clinch to make wampum.

Dress It Up

For Him:
* Cowboy hat
* Leather cowboy boots
* Checked shirt
* Dungarees
* Bandana
* Fake gun or lasso

For Her:
* Warpaint
* Children's toy bow and arrows
* Head-dress
* Leather fringed dress
* Moccasins

Make It Real
Finish by snuggling up
in front of a campfire.

XXX Rating
She might
not dare
scalp him, but
she can give him
a close shave using a
regular razor. He might
return the favour,
scalping a different
part of her body.

SCENE 4 Have You Been *Naughty* or *Nice*?

Basic Plot
Ho! Ho! Ho! Apparently, one in five women has a
secret fantasy to get jolly with Santa Claus.

Getting It On Game for Newbies
It's the night before Christmas and all through the
house, Santa is stirring and getting ready to rouse.
She finds her secret Santa waiting in the lounge,
slides on to his lap and, when he asks what
she wants for Christmas, snuggles in close and
whispers her lustiest holiday list. He's happy to
slip her whatever she desires.

Getting It On Game for Experienced Scenesters
Christmas is the time of giving more than receiving. Wearing
a red or silver velvet gown with nothing underneath but red
garters, she invites Santa to unwrap her. Afterwards, she licks
his candy cane until it is sticky.

Getting It On Game for Hardcore Role-Players
She is extra naughty and teases Santa like
a vixen – jingling his bells and decorating
his balls but never quite banging his
cracker. He decides she is a very bad girl
indeed and needs a spanking.

Dress It Up

For Him:
* Santa suit
* White beard

For Her:
* Long red or silver velvet robe
* Red garters

Make It Real

Put on a stack of Christmas tunes. She can write to Santa, telling him all the "presents" she wants him to give to her.

XXX Rating

Santa should have a sack of goodies such as cinnamon-scented lube, a soft paddle, a vibrator that syncs to your mobile, red velvet nipple clamps or handcuffs.

SCENE 5 The Belly Dancer

Basic Plot
She makes him dance to her tunes
with her seductive moves.

Getting It On Game for Newbies

Set up some cushions for him to recline on. Put on some Arabic music. She then dances into the room with a veil covering her face and draped in scarves, jingling as she moves. She approaches the Sheik, shaking her hips. If he reaches out to grab them, she should lightly slap his hands and tell him no as she shakes her finger.

She circles the room, takes off a scarf and, placing it over his eyes, gives him a passionate kiss before dancing away. The next time, she takes a scarf and lightly uses it to give him a quick caress between his legs. This touch-and-go dancing continues until she has removed all of her scarves.

She removes her top and shakes her breasts, coming oh-so-close to him. When he tries to touch her, she smiles and dances away. Finally, she takes his hands and places them on her hips and she dances for a few minutes before shimmying onto the cushions.

Getting It On Game for Experienced Scenesters

She should kneel and, shimmying and shaking, lean all the way back until she is doing a backbend (this is only for the supple). Don't expect him to wait for the seventh veil to come off in this position.

Getting It On Game for Hardcore Role-Players

She can invite her Sheik to remove her scarves with his teeth, letting him kiss and nuzzle her as she gradually unveils more flesh. Once she is naked, you can both make love to the pulsating rhythm of the music. When it beats fast make love with passion and when it beats slow take your time.

Dress It Up

For Him:
* Long white or striped robe
* White headpiece
* Dark sunglasses

For Her:
* Short top that shows your belly button
* Long silky skirt
* Lots of scarves
* Jingly ankle bracelets
* Hoop earrings
* Lots of bangles
* Silk veil

XXX Rating
Include a groin-shaking (and groan-inducing) dance in his lap.

Make It Real
Watch a belly-dancing DVD to get the right moves.

 # SCENE 6 HOT COP

Basic Plot
What will you do to get out of this speeding ticket?

 ### Getting It On Game for Newbies
He sits in "the driver's seat". She saunters up in her raunchy cop's uniform, ready to throw the book at him. He offers to do anything to avoid getting ticketed. She takes him up on his offer, telling him to "spread 'em".

 ### Getting It On Game for Experienced Scenesters
He runs to avoid arrest. She gives chase, catching him in the bedroom. She sternly tells him he is being arrested for carrying a deadly weapon, cuffs his hands behind his back and reads him his rights. She then plays with his "gun" until it "accidentally" goes off.

 ### Getting It On Game for Hardcore Role-Players
Who's been a naughty boy? That's right: someone needs a lesson in police procedure! Designate an area as the "cells". She leads her "prisoner" there. Thrilling to the idea that he is under her control, she tells him he is entirely in her hands – there's no calling his lawyer this time! She removes his belt and shoelaces and then strip-searches him. Because he is a deviant criminal, she decides to keep him in solitary confinement until he serves his time.

Dress It Up

For Him:
* Belted trousers
* Shoes with laces

For Her:
* Cop's hat
* Sexy police uniform
* Fake gun/night stick
* Handcuffs
* Ticket book
* Police sunglasses
* Shield

Make It Real

She politely refers to him as "Sir" the entire time and keeps her voice deadpan.

XXX Rating

In the ticket book, she can write various "punishments" – 20 minutes of lip service, a one-hour rub down, receiver's choice and so on...

SCENE 7 *Starring Role*

Basic Plot
It's movie night!

 Getting It On Game for Newbies

Send yourselves an invitation to a costume party. You and your guest are asked to wear matching costumes. But it's a week before Halloween and all the costumes have been picked through. You have no choice but to go as (insert favourite movie personalities). Once you are geared up, act out your top movie scenes with these characters – then rewrite the scripts to include an especially exciting climax.

 **Getting It On Game for Experienced Scenesters**

Don't bother with the party invites – challenge yourselves to a weekend of living as your characters.

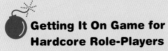 **Getting It On Game for Hardcore Role-Players**

Throw a costume party yourselves. Mid-revelry, slip off to act out your own thrilling adventure – just make sure you grab the right character to rehearse with!

Dress It Up

Top-rated XXX couples for scenesters:

* Hans Solo and Princess Leia
* Batman and Catwoman
* Superman and Wonder Woman
* Captain Kirk or Picard and a female Klingon or Vulcan (how can you tell?)
* Tarzan and Jane

XXX Rating
Instead of getting the actual costume,
splash out for the sex shop versions, which
will have handy openings and come with
titillating accessories such as a vibrating light
sabre or leather cat-o-nine tails.

Make It Real
Use actual scripts from the movies (www.imsdb.com
and www.simplyscripts.com) are good sources for
loads of free online scripts).

SCENE 8 ROMAN ROMP

Basic Plot
Take a trip back to ancient Rome
for a night of decadent loving.

Getting It On Game for Newbies
Begin your orgy of pleasure by planning to while away the day
in the bath. Fill the tub with warm water and mix in a cupful of
scented oil. Take it in turns to soak in the perfumed water or, if
the tub is big enough, bathe together. Make it a really sensual
experience, languorously washing every inch of your partner's
body with large sponges soaked alternately in hot and cold
water. Feed each other grapes and drink large goblets of wine.
Once you are completely clean, ravage each other dirty again.

Getting It On Game for Experienced Scenesters
Slather yourselves in oil and nude
wrestle. The loser gives the winner
some thumb's up action.

Getting It On Game for Hardcore Role-players
Slip into a toga (nothing underneath,
obviously). Drape it so that all it takes is
a simple tug to hail each other's Caesar.
See how many positions you can do
reclining on a bed of cushions.

Dress It Up

HIM:
* Sheet for toga
* Vine crown
* Simple leather sandals

HER:
* Jewels to wear in her hair
* Sheet for toga
* Small tiara
* Simple leather sandals

XXX Rating
Turn it into a feast of pleasure – eat food from one another's body, try passing the wine from one mouth to another without spilling a drop, or catch grapes in your mouths (if you miss, you perform a forfeit).

Make It Real
Once dressed, indulge in a great feast. Romans ate their meals while lolling on couches (slaves sat at the table, ready to "serve"). Make sure there is plenty of fresh fruit – peaches, pineapples, pomegranates, passion fruit, figs and, of course, juicy grapes – to feed each other.

Chapter Two

At Your Service

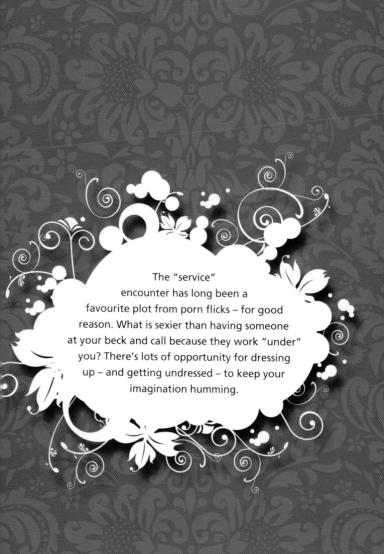

The "service" encounter has long been a favourite plot from porn flicks – for good reason. What is sexier than having someone at your beck and call because they work "under" you? There's lots of opportunity for dressing up – and getting undressed – to keep your imagination humming.

SCENE 9 *EXPRESS SERVICE*

Basic Plot
She has a crush on the delivery man and has been dying to check out his package.

Getting It On Game for Newbies
The deliveryman usually leaves the boxes and knocks on the door before he gets back in his truck and drives away. This time she plans to catch him and seduce him. She dresses in her sexiest lingerie. When he drives up, she tells him she has a tip and invites him in. She closes the door and gives him some lip service.

Getting It On Game for Experienced Scenesters
He tells her he has a route to finish. She says that she doesn't care and that she has a special parcel for him. Slipping out of her lingerie, she strikes a seductive pose and asks him if he thinks he can deliver.

Getting It On Game for Hardcore Role-players
Tell him that it's an express service and he has five minutes to wrap things up.

Dress It Up

For Him:
* Any sort of delivery outfit will do
* A box or two (see Make It Real)

For Her:
* Skimpy lingerie

Make It Real

Order up some sex toys by post about a week before you plan to play. Don't open it when it arrives – he can use the box as his prop when he makes his delivery.

XXX Rating

Tear open your package and use what's inside to send each other to orgasm island.

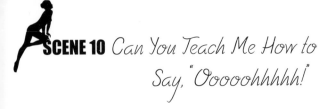

SCENE 10 Can You Teach Me How to Say, "Ooooohhhhh!"

Basic Plot

You'll both learn something sweet new tricks when you play at being a sex instructor and client.

Getting It On Game for Newbies

He has problems controlling his rifle and tends to shoot too quickly. So he pays a visit to a sex instructor. She manhandles his weapon, showing him different ways to hold fire. When he's ready to lock and load, she takes aim and gives a final squeeze.

Getting It On Game for Experienced Scenesters

She has a shelf full of reference material – new ways to play with each other and get into position. She picks a few out for them to work on now.

Getting It On Game for
Hardcore Role-players

She creates a worksheet (or gives him a book or worksheet) on various sexual techniques such as kissing, touching, massage, oral sex, and so on, including a specific rating system. She tells him that he is taking a pop quiz and she has him perform each technique to the best of his ability, scoring him based on the rating system. His homework is any technique for which he receives a low grade. He will be given an oral exam in a few days.

Before the "quiz date" she should look over the work she gave her partner and assign a point value to each position. Make a position that you both already know or that you're not terribly interested in worth one point. Positions she'd like to try or that interests her should be worth two points. Make positions she thinks they'll never be able to remember or do worth three points. When it's time to quiz, she let's him know that if he gets enough points she'll do him a sensual favour. If not, he has to perform one for her.

Dress It Up

For Him:
* A hospital gown

For Her:
* A white lab coat

Make It Real

She should medi-speak the correct names for things as much as possible: "penile dysfunction", "premature ejaculation", "cunnilingus", "fellatio", "vulva", "clitoris" and so on.

XXX Rating

Instead of pencils in her pocket, she can carry a thin vibrator, a penis clamp and other delicious implements of pleasure. Around her neck, instead of a stethoscope, she can have anal beads.

SCENE 11 Book Club

Basic Plot
She is a typical prim librarian – hair up in a tight bun, plain clothes and oversized glasses. He is checking out a book.

Getting It On Game for Newbies
She is sitting behind a desk. He comes up to check out a book and she removes her glasses and undoes her hair, revealing the sexy heroine that she really is. She then leans over and gives him a lusty smack on the lips. He is so surprised, he drops the books on the floor. The two of you climb on the desk and write your own sexy plot.

Getting It On Game for Experienced Scenesters
No groaning or moaning allowed – after all, this is a library and you must keep quiet.

Getting It On Game for Hardcore Role-Players
Part of the allure of the librarian is the smart sex, so as he takes her on the desk, she whispers carnal tidbits in his ear: "Approximately one million orgasms happen daily"; "'Pussy' and 'tits' are the most searched words on the internet"; "An orgasm is one of the best cures for a headache."

Dress It Up

For Her:
* Tight pencil skirt
* Button-down shirt
* Horn-rimmed glasses
* Hair in a tight bun
* Sensible pumps
* A barely-there slip and thong

XXX Rating
Pick up a stack of sexy how-to books to use as reference while you play.

Make It Real
She should use proper grammar and a large vocabulary throughout – so instead of "Take me now!" she cries, "Let us culminate with intercourse!"

SCENE 12 *Artistic Vision*

Basic Plot
**One of you is an artist or photographer creating
a piece of art from the other's nude model.**

Getting It On Game for Newbies

Don't worry about having any talent. This is just an excuse to study your lover long and hard. The artist sets up their sketch pad and instructs the model to pose exactly how they want. They can do whatever they want with the model for "art's sake", telling them how to stand and pose with whatever props you have to hand.

Getting It On Game for Experienced Scenesters

The artist tells their model to play with themselves, saying that they want to sketch their orgasm.

Getting It On Game for Hardcore Role-Players

Switch to video and keep the camera running even after you live up to your randy reputations as artistic types and make wild beautiful love on the studio floor.

Dress It Up

For Him:
* Loose white shirt
* Baggy trousers

For Her:
* Black shirt
* Black leggings

XXX Rating
Experiment with different positions that leave nothing to the imagination.

Make It Real
Lighting is incredibly important. Keep it low and flattering to avoid the looking like you are making *Art Attack* or *Vincent Van Grow* (unless that is the storyline you are creating).

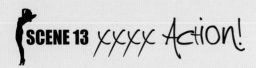

SCENE 13 XXXX Action!

Basic Plot
He is a porn director filming his favourite actress.

Getting It On Game for Newbies

He gives her very precise directions on how to pleasure herself. Make sure she has a real orgasm – viewers can always tell when it's fake.

Getting It On Game for Experienced Scenesters

It's the money shot – after watching her work at herself for awhile, he decides to get in on the action. She closes her eyes and pretends that there are four other well-endowed studs waiting in line. To help him out, he can use a vibrator and butt plug to simulate many hands making light work.

Getting It On Game for Hardcore Role-Players

Any porn flick worth its rating has some girl-on-girl action. If you don't want to invite a third party to your games, invest in the Clit Kisser, a sex toy that simulates cunnilingus (see pages 10–12 and 127 for resources).

Dress It Up

For Him:
* Tight shirt
* Tighter trousers

For Her:
* Any over-the-top lingerie

XXX Rating
Break out the camera and film the action for real.

Make It Real
She should come up with a porn moniker such as "Bambi" or "Busty Barbie" to perform under.

SCENE 14 Healthy Check-Up

Basic Plot
She makes his temperature rise by playing nurse
and giving a saucy head-to-toe examination.

Getting It On Game for Newbies

She greets him and leads him into the bedroom, telling
him to climb onto the table (the bed) get completely
undressed and put on a hospital gown. She starts nuzzling
him, telling him she's testing his blood pressure. She then
strokes him, saying she is seeing how sensitive he is to
touch before checking his pulse. Hopefully it's racing.
Worried, she says that she really should take a sample –
and works his test tube to squeeze one out. She finishes
by reminding him to take his medicine (one orgasm daily).

Getting It On Game for Experienced Scenesters

She tells him that she has a test the next day on the male
anatomy and asks if she can use his for study purposes.

Getting It On Game for Hardcore Role-Players

She tells him she needs to take his
temperature the old-fashioned way and slips
a small vibrator or butt plug up his bottom.
She exclaims that he has a temperature and
the only way to cure it is to make him sweat
– and then she proceeds to do just that.

Dress It Up

For Him:
* Hospital gown

For Her:
* Sexy PVC nurse uniform
* Stethoscope
* Nurse cap

XXX Rating

She can carry a doctor's bag full of sex toys that she can use during the exam – polyurethane gloves, small vibrators, massage oils and butt plugs.

Make It Real

She should warm her hands before starting to examine him.

SCENE 15 *Private Dancer*

Basic Plot
Put on your own private show.

Getting It On Game for Newbies

She is a stripper in a private club and paid to give a solo show. She turns on the music, dims the lights and starts moving. Because she is a pro, she knows that the emphasis is on "teasing" rather than "stripping" (she can check out Carmen Electra's *Aerobic Striptease* DVD for inspiration). The rules: While dancing, she can touch him, rub against him, kiss him, rub her breasts or bottom in his face, tease him with her tongue, sit in his lap facing him with her legs wrapped around him, sit in his lap backwards and squirm her bottom back and forth, whatever he wants... Basically, absolutely anything goes her end. However, under no circumstances is he allowed to touch her or remove his clothes.

Getting It On Game for Experienced Scenesters

He's trying his best to hook up with her after she's finished dancing and this is her last set, so he doesn't have much time. He tries flirting with her, complimenting her, sliding money into her garter or G-string or whatever she has on. She leans down and takes the money out of his mouth with hers, turning around and throwing it to the floor on her "stage" like they do at a Gentleman's Club. Or she holds her breasts and lets him put the bill in between, pushing them together. She then turns and struts off before slowly turning and beckoning to him.

Getting It On Game for Hardcore Role-Players

She stages a grand finale. She lies down on her back, arching her pelvis into the air. Sliding her hands seductively down the sides of her belly, teasingly tracing around her bellybutton, she then slides her hand into her panties (if they are still on) and begins shamelessly masturbating to the music (she can work some toys in here if she wants). After she's put a smile on her face, she goes back to him, kneels in front of his chair, unzips his trousers and takes his mini pole out for its own striptease.

Dress It Up

For Him:
* A thong underneath business clothes in case you decide to switch roles

For Her:
* Clothes she can get out of easily and gracefully
* Stilettos as high as she can stand without falling over
* Matching bra, panties and garter
* Stockings, preferably fishnets
* Elbow-length gloves
* Sexy dress, robe or man's shirt to wear on top
* Feather boa or long necklace
* Belly chain
* Body glitter

XXX Rating
Work with a stripper pole – you can get them from a sex toy shop (see pages 10–12 and 127) or make a simple one out of PVC pipe.

Make It Real
Make sure he is loaded up with paper currency to show his appreciation.

SCENE 16 *Down & Dirty, Oo La La*

Basic Plot
Turn housework into play time with a little
je ne sais quoi and a frisky French outfit.

Getting It On Game for Newbies
She goes into the bedroom before him and starts lightly
dusting the furniture. When he comes in a few moments
later, she says in a French accent, "Oh, *s'il vous plaît*, so
sorry, I was given permission to take extra time to do an
extra special job." She then you looks him over and says,
"Pardon, monsieur, your clothes are so dirtee. Let me
remove them for you." Before long, the door handles
are not the only knobs she is polishing.

Getting It On Game for Experienced Scenesters
He doesn't wait for her to give him a rubdown. Being a good
servant, she doesn't protest when he throws her down on the
bed and takes her. Still playing the sub (submissive), she offers
to wash him down in the shower afterwards.

Getting It On Game for Hardcore Role-Players
Zut alors! She is a saucy French maid
who ties her master to the bed and
teases him with a feather duster for
leaving his socks on the floor.

Dress It Up

For Him:
* Something elegant such as a suit and tie or a tux

For Her:
* Short black dress, usually with a lacy or fluffy crinoline underneath and white trim
* Small white apron
* Tiny hat
* Black seamed stockings

XXX Rating
Take your action out of the house – rent a hotel room to play in.

Make It Real
Speak your lines in *ze* French accent.

Chapter Three

True Romance

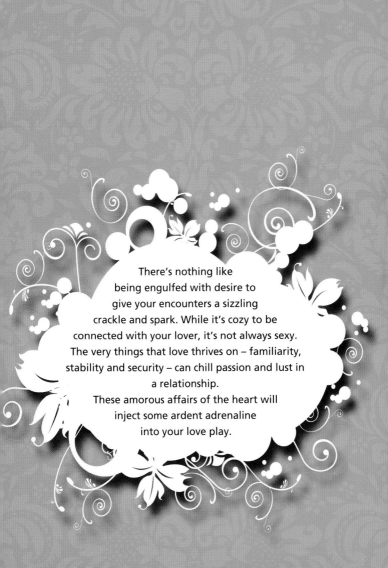

There's nothing like
being engulfed with desire to
give your encounters a sizzling
crackle and spark. While it's cozy to be
connected with your lover, it's not always sexy.
The very things that love thrives on – familiarity,
stability and security – can chill passion and lust in
a relationship.
These amorous affairs of the heart will
inject some ardent adrenaline
into your love play.

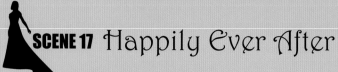

SCENE 17 *Happily Ever After*

Basic Plot
Who doesn't dream of a fairytale
ending to the randy rendezvous?

Getting It On Game for Newbies

Sleeping Beauty is in a deep sleep so she lies down on the
bed (a couch will also do), eyes closed. Along comes Prince
Charming, ready to rescue her. He knows a simple kiss
will just not be enough to break the spell and awaken her.
Kneeling next to her, he opens her bodice and bra and then
lightly caresses her chest to make sure she is still breathing.
He continues to work his way down, down, down, stroking
her body with his fingers. He slides down her knickers and,
spreading her legs, rubs her treasure spot until she begins
to moan. His princess is awake.

Getting It On Game for Experienced Scenesters

Sleeping Beauty opens her eyes and breathes, "My Prince!" She sees
the bulge between his legs and invites him to release his royal sabre.

Getting It On Game for Hardcore Role-Players

Alas! She is no sweet princess – she is the wicked queen. She
puts a spell on him and makes him her private sex slave. He
must service her every need, desire and whim for 40 years (or
else she will turn him into a frog).

Dress It Up

For Him:
* Crown
* Breeches or leggings
* Velvet purple or burgundy cape
* White silky, blousy shirt
* (Fake) sword
* High boots

For Her:
* Silky gown that opens at the front
* Slippers
* Crown
* Sexy bra and underwear

XXX Rating

Instead of awakening her with a caress, Prince Charming brings Sleeping Beauty back to life with a kiss to her nether regions.

Make It Real

Study the fairytale and use actual language from the plot.

SCENE 18 *Bedroom Idol*

Basic Plot
It's your lucky night as your favourite Hollywood hottie of the moment (or a hunka-hunka fusion of as many celebs as you lust for) makes a star appearance in your bed.

Getting It On Game for Newbies
Your star sweetie is making a movie and you have a backstage pass. You sneak into their trailer (your bedroom) and, taking off your clothes, lie in wait as a guest surprise.

Getting It On Game for Experienced Scenesters
You have a nude love scene with your fantasy pin-up. You are nervous because you have never done this before but they promise you won't even have to act.

Getting It On Game for Hardcore Role-Players
Your celeb is no McHollywood icon – instead, he or she is a top-tier porn star. You play out scenes from their most hardcore off-the-wall, on-the-couch, under-the-bed, in-the-restroom, up-a-tree-in, on-a-car action. (Check online for the top 100 adult films of all time at www.gamelink.com.)

Dress It Up

* If you are the celeb, check out a gossip mag for inspiration

* If you are the star-struck groupie, everyday clothes will do

Make It Real
Reenact a sex scene that your dream lover has actually played in.

XXX Rating
Log onto www.celebritysexfantasy.com for adult movies starring your favourite lookalike celebs.

SCENE 19 *Close-Ups*

Basic Plot
Get inspired by cinema's hottest love scenes.

 Getting It On Game for Newbies

The movie scenes women find most exciting deal with emotional connection and gazing into each other's eyes, while men get off on the ones where they can see some skin. Here are seven that work for both sides of the aisle:

The Big Easy: The awkward stop-and-start pacing and preference for dialogue over heavy breathing will please her while Ellen Barkin's orgasm will satisfy him.

Titanic: She'll get hot and bothered by the doomed young couple love story while he'll appreciate Kate Winslet showing how to make a rumble seat really rumble.

Shakespeare in Love: She'll be primed from literary love while he will be Gwyneth Paltrow's Bard-core moment.

Thelma and Louise: Her heart will be stolen by Brad Pitt – and so will his.

Bull Durham: You'll both make a home-run as a pedicure turns into a passionate treatment in full-body sex.

Ghost: She'll get horny weeping over doomed love while his artistic side will appreciate some messy, clay-covered sex.

Stealing Beauty: You'll both play and replay the scene where Liv Tyler loses her virginity to a sexy young Italian boy.

⚡ Getting It On Game for Experienced Scenesters

The best movie sex depend on the surprise, the strangeness, the thrilling newness of a steamy encounter out of your usual environs. These seven impromptu hot-and-heavy interludes will all tap your risqué, reckless feeling of "We might get caught, but who cares?" exhibitionist streak.

1 The kitchen sink moment in *Fatal Attraction*
2 Against the wall in *Sea of Love*
3 In the restaurant bathroom in *Unfaithful*
4 On a train in *Risky Business*
5 Halfway up the stairs in *A History of Violence* (bonus moment: teenage cheerleading role-play sex)
6 In a limo (although a car will do) in *No Way Out*
7 In the pool, at the carwash (is there anywhere these three don't do it?) in *Wild Things*

Getting It On Game for Hardcore Role-Players

Onscreen sex scenes tend to get really hot when they depict something kinky. Five movies to ring your raunch bell:

1 *Something Wild* breaks out the handcuffs but he can loosely tie her wrists with a silk or velvet scarf if you don't want to bond under lock and key.

2 *Last Tango in Paris* uses butter but you can feed your fantasies with any food or even an ice cube.

3 *Body of Evidence* shows what else candles are good for besides providing romantic lighting.

4 *Basic Instinct* is a primer in how to flash a roomful of men – or just that special someone – without catching a draft.

5 *Emmanuelle* will spur you on to put your sexual fantasies to good use.

Dress It Up

✳ Use the film as your
inspiration for how you
dress (see pages 10–12
for ideas on where to
get different period
costumes).

Make It Real

Set an Oscar-worthy scene – movie sex is
orchestrated to the very last detail. You don't have
to redecorate but you can tidy up to create a high-
octane erotic charge in your home. None of Keira
Knightley's characters would make love in a bedroom
cluttered with bills, a Thighmaster and photos of
your cat, and neither should you. Boudoir staples
really do work – satin sheets, flickering candles and
filmy curtains swirling in the breeze (much sexier
than miniblinds). Same goes for whatever room
you end up in – surrounding the bath with candles,
dimming the lighting in the lounge or cleaning the
remnants of dinner off of the dining table will give
your scene star quality.

XXX Rating

Some of the raciest sex scenes come from the chemistry of a clean-cut guy and a bossy vixen revved up and ready to roll into bed. Even if you are not hardwired to act this way, there are plenty of little ways to unleash the sex symbol within and leave him feeling blissfully ravished – you can flirt with him, using girlie moves like twirling your hair or stroking your neck, or pull a "helpless little me" move and ask for his help putting on your bra and shirt. Or use sound effects with lots of groans, moans, sighs and take-me-now's.

SCENE 20 *Royal Moments*

Basic Plot
She is a damsel in distress, running away from her evil
stepmother queen. He is her knight in shining armour.

Getting It On Game for Newbies

Turn your home into a castle by draping lots of cloth and
tapestry around. She bangs on the front door, looking to
escape the horsemen who have been ordered to kill her. He
lets her in and, seeing that she is chilled, begins to rub her
down. Gradually, he heats her up to the point where she
loses her royal composure.

Getting It On Game for Experienced Scenesters

Seeing that time is of essence, he tells
her to jump on his steed and he will
take her away. She sits on his lap and
they ride at a fast pace.

Getting It On Game for Hardcore Role-Players

He is in cahoots with her stepmother. He brings her "down"
to his dungeon, which is kitted out in instruments of torture
(handcuffs, light whip, nipple clamps, etc). He turns her into
his sex slave.

Dress It Up

For Him:
* High boots
* (Fake) sword
* Snood
* Vest
* Leggings

For Her:
* Gown
* Crown

XXX Rating
Doubting her purity, he can put a chastity belt on her (see pages 10–12 and 127 for resources).

Make It Real
He can invest in chain mail tunic, available from costume supply stores.

Chapter Four

Stranger Danger

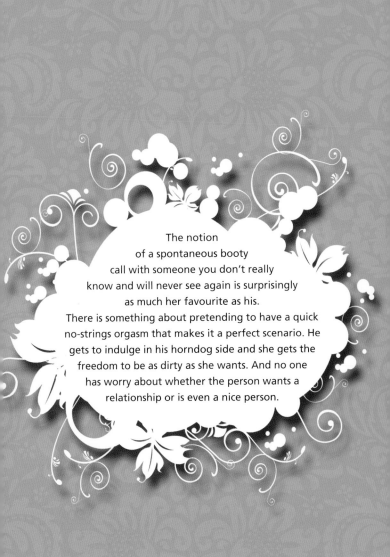

The notion
of a spontaneous booty
call with someone you don't really
know and will never see again is surprisingly
as much her favourite as his.
There is something about pretending to have a quick
no-strings orgasm that makes it a perfect scenario. He
gets to indulge in his horndog side and she gets the
freedom to be as dirty as she wants. And no one
has worry about whether the person wants a
relationship or is even a nice person.

Basic Plot
She's the horny housewife who calls a
plumber to fix her (ahem) pipes.

Getting It On Game for Newbies

She answers the door in a sheer nightie, saying she's only just
woken up. She leads him to the bathroom, saying the shower
or bath isn't working and she just can't wait to get wet but that
she doesn't have any money to pay him so perhaps they can
work something out. He is more than happy to let her play with
his "tools" and do some twisting on his pipe.

Getting It On Game for Experienced Scenesters

Since you're in the bathroom,
introduce some water play. Test
out the bubble bath to make sure it
works properly or, if you have one,
see how much pressure you can get
out of the handheld sprayer.

Getting It On Game for Hardcore Role-Players

He has special equipment in his toolbox – grease (lube) to help
those pipes slide together, soap (or whipped cream) to coat
whatever you will and a tiny screwdriver (vibrator) to tighten
leaky nuts and bolts.

Dress It Up

For Him:
* Plumber uniform – don't forget to stitch your name above the pocket

For Her:
* A sheer negligée

XXX Rating
Turn your play into a dom/sub moment by making him the "Master Plumber".

Make It Real
Make up a business card with a list of the "services" you offer, available 24 hours.

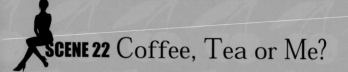

SCENE 22 Coffee, Tea or Me?

Basic Plot
Get ready to serve up some passion on a platter
when she dresses up as a full-service hostess
with the mostess.

Getting It On Game for Newbies

Have a table set. When he arrives, he should greet her
by her waitress name (it's written on a badge on her
shirt). She seats him at a candlelit table covered in a
crisp white tablecloth. She places a napkin on his lap,
carefully smoothing it down and making sure it covers
everything. She then begins to recite the night's
specials, such as a two-minute lap dance, a back
massage, a mini striptease or a full-body massage.
She asks if he wants a tasting menu or if he wants to
order à la carte. Create a menu of fun and flirty treats
your partner can order.

Getting It On Game for
Experienced Scenesters

The customer is always right so he
gets to order special off-menu items.
Her tip will be based on how well
she "serves" them.

Getting It On
Game for Hardcore
Role-Players

She turns him into the *plat du jour*. She covers his chest and all the way down and around his penis with whipped cream and not-too-hot fudge. Then she places strawberries randomly over his chest and slowly eats each one before licking the sticky sauces off.

Make It Real

She should serve up some
sensual foods to feed him:

- Grapes
- Bananas
- Champagne
- Strawberries
- Chocolate
- Oysters
- Whipped Cream

Dress It Up

For Him:
* Evening clothes

For Her:
* A short plain black dress
* A frilly white apron
* A lacy headscarf or hanky
  for a hat

XXX Rating
She can serve him
nyotaimori, or "naked sushi". She
lies naked with sushi adorning her
body which he then eats directly off
of her (search google images for a
visual on this one).

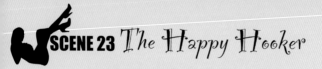

SCENE 23 *The Happy Hooker*

Basic Plot
He's looking for some sex on the wild side and
willing to pay for it. She's on the game.

Getting It On Game for Newbies

Wearing nothing more than a skimpy bra, panties, high heels and a
long coat, she approaches his car. Letting her coat hang open to give
him a flash of what's underneath, she leans over and asks him if he
wants some action. He asks how much. She replies she gets paid by
the act – so much for a BJ, more for full sex, anal sex and so on and
asks what his pleasure is tonight. Being hardnosed, she makes sure
he pays upfront. Then you both go home so you can give him his
money's worth (keeping those heels on!).

Getting It On Game for Experienced Scenesters

Instead of taking the action home, head to a cheap hotel
that you can rent by the hour. Don't forget to hang the Do
Not Disturb sign. She can keep the play going by talking
dirty throughout (Tip: it sounds sexier when you use a lower
octave and talk slower than you normally would).

Getting It On Game for Hardcore Role-Players

Don't bother with a hotel room. The ultimate fantasy for most
guys is to get a no-strings-attached blowjob. She can work south
of his border right there in the car or find a back alleyway.

Dress It Up

For Him:
* Suit and tie

For Her:
* Sexy bra
* Thong
* Long belted coat
* Wig
* High heels

XXX Rating
He is paying so he feels comfortable asking for something he normally never would – like backdoor sex.

Make It Real
No kissing allowed.

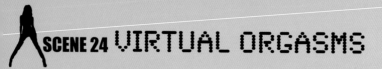

Basic Plot

Different from porn, which is all about the money shot, cyber games are a risk-free way to flirt with different randy roles via your computer.

Getting It On Game for Newbies

In the world of erotic video games, there are loads of virtual sex games and they all treat it a little differently, but here are some steps, tips and tricks to get you started.

You'll need:
- Disc-based game
- Computer
- Downloaded game file
- Major console

Find a site that intrigues you. The biggest are Sims (www.thesims2.ea.com), Sociolotron SM (www.sociolotron.amerabyte.com), Playskins (www.playskins.com), and Second Life. Each online role-playing game (RPG) is a bit different – some are all about the sex; others just include sex. Test out a few before you commit (some have monthly fees that allow you to play for a while and quit if you do not like them). In some games, nudity and sexual behaviour are forbidden outside private areas and sex clubs.

Create your character.

Get familiar with your virtual universe. Learn the rules of the game and the conventions of game play. You can sit back and observe to see how others interact and build on their models.

Start making virtual friends. You'll soon find a character you click with.

Make some nano nookie. Use suggestive language to segue into virtual sex, and then proceed with whatever the game allows.

> **Getting It On Game for Experienced Scenesters**
> Don't just chat about sex. You can buy outfits to dress your avatars provocatively, or "skins" to make them appear nude. In some games, you may also need to purchase your avatar's genitals.

> **Getting It On Game for Hardcore Role-Players**
> Once you have the look and voice of your avatar down, buy equipment, ranging from realistic-looking beds and other furniture to fanciful torture devices used in BDSM fantasies.

Dress It Up

* You can be as dressed or undressed as you desire

XXX Rating
Have real sex virtually – guys can get a virtual sex stroker for the penis while cyber babes can try out the virtual vibrator.

Make It Real

Be extremely wary of meeting in real life anybody you encounter online. This is especially true if you met them in a virtual sex game.

SCENE 25 Someone to Watch Over Me

Basic Plot

Pretending that you're being watched while you get it on is erotic, exhilarating and slightly taboo.

Getting It On Game for Newbies

Dress in front-opening clothing to make undressing just that more intriguing. One of you stands while the other is across the room in the shadows, sitting in a chair. The stander pretends that they are alone and feeling lusty. They are thinking lewd thoughts when they notice the sitter watching. They decide to give them a show. Slowly, they remove their clothes and begin playing with themselves. The watcher shouldn't talk or touch them.

Getting It On Game for Experienced Scenesters

Notch up the action by imaging you are getting it on with the neighbour. Call them by name as much as possible, saying how much you like the way they are touching you and how you hope (name your lover) doesn't catch you together.

Getting It On Game for Hardcore Role-Players

Take your show on the road. You and pretend neighbour do it outside or in the car parked in front of the house, or in any potential danger spot where you just might be seen doing your dirty deed.

Dress It Up

For Him:
* Buttoned jeans
* Buttoned shirt

For Her:
* Buttoned shirt
* A front-opening bra
* Long hitch-it-high skirt

Make It Real
Make up a new nickname for your pretend lover.

XXX Rating
Doing it in front of the window that faces your neighbour's house will make your sexual worlds collide into an orgasmic frenzy.

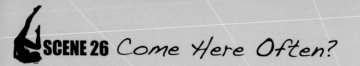
SCENE 26 *Come Here Often?*

Basic Plot

Two strangers meet and (wantonly) greet each other.

 Getting It On Game for Newbies

It doesn't take a lot of work to recapture that "just-met" excitement. Go back to being strangers by re-enacting your first-ever meeting or date, maybe even returning to the scene of the crime. Think about what you were wearing at the time, what your hair looked like. If you can't make it the exact place, try for somewhere similar (fancy restaurant, park, party).

When you do finally get horizontal, treat each other's bodies like brand-new-never-tried-before playthings – try and (re)discover what you both like, relish the unfamiliar scent of your bodies and taste of your skin. These small details will fire up that tear-each-other's-clothes-off desire you had when you started to get to know each other.

⚡ Getting It On Game for Experienced Scenesters

Forget your past and create a new history together. Both of you go to a bar or party – separately. Once there, act as if you don't know each other (a makeover, like a new outfit or hairdo, will make it easier to get into character as will a brand-new name). He sends a drink over to her and then walks over and introduces himself. You make small talk (don't even try to be truthful about yourself) and start flirting – casually touching each other, locking eyes and, if you dare, lips. She can up the ante by leaving off her panties and giving him a flash of what's (not) underneath. She turbocharges the thrill of the chase by playing hard to get, acting coy when he suggests she come back to his place. Even in the height of ecstasy, keep on using your pretend names.

Getting It On Game for Hardcore Role-Players

Take your scene out on the road. One of you stands on the side of the road hitching and lets the other pick you up. Then find a secluded parking lot where you can get naughty.

Dress It Up

For Him:
* Something brand new that she has never seen you in and different from your usual style

For Her:
* Wig
* Something brand new that he has never seen you in and different from your usual style

XXX Rating
Blindfolding yourselves and taking turns lightly kissing each other's bodies or stroking each other's skin with your fingertips will make you feel naughty-new all over. You may be surprised at how many extra sensations you've been missing all this time.

Make It Real
To recapture that just-met sizzle, you have to snap out of the same-old sex routine. Step out of your comfort zone with something different from your usual – a different position, sex with the lights on (or off), getting more vocal, or pretending to forget their name in the morning.

Chapter Five
At the Controls

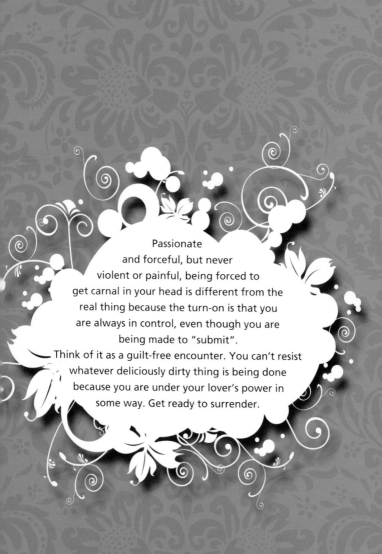

Passionate and forceful, but never violent or painful, being forced to get carnal in your head is different from the real thing because the turn-on is that you are always in control, even though you are being made to "submit".

Think of it as a guilt-free encounter. You can't resist whatever deliciously dirty thing is being done because you are under your lover's power in some way. Get ready to surrender.

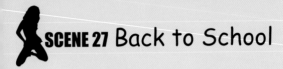

SCENE 27 Back to School

Basic Plot
No matter how experienced you both are at your lusty
A B Cs, he can always give her a lesson in love.

Getting It On Game for Newbies
She approaches him, holding some books and says, "Excuse me,
Mr _____, I was wondering if you had time to help me with
this homework?" From now on, he will take the lead, enticing
her by stroking her through her clothing, gently playing with her
nipples through the fabric and rubbing his fingers between her
legs. When she is squirming, he takes off each piece, one by one,
continuing to fondle her, until she is standing naked before him.
He can assure her that everything will be fine and that he will
give her lots of pleasure, using phrases such as "I'll be gentle",
"Relax, please" and "I'll make you feel really good".

Getting It On Game for Experienced Scenesters
She resists his attempts to touch her
or take off her clothes, but finally gives
in to his seductive touch, all the while
murmuring sweet innocent phrases like
"Don't do it", "I am so afraid", "Please
be gentle". When the final moment
comes, he lies her down on the bed and
oh-so-gently slides in, inch by inch.

Getting It On Game for Hardcore Role-Players

She innocently tempts him. She moves a chair across from him and sits, legs slightly spread and ankles crossed – which lets him have a peak of her white knickers and what's to come. She says it's hot in his office and unbuttons her blouse a bit, showing off the simple bra below. When he starts getting a little too frisky, she stops him, saying she has never been with anyone before, admitting that she sometimes masturbates thinking of him. He asks if he can watch her. After touching herself for a few minutes, she opens wide, saying she has always fantasized about him touching her "down there".

Dress It Up

For Him:
* Suit and tie

For Her:
* White button-up blouse
* Classic plaid or plain pleated schoolgirl skirt
* White briefs or children's character knickers
* Simple white bra
* Loafers

XXX Rating
Once "deflowered", she can become a naughty schoolgirl and bind him up with his own tie.

Make It Real
She can put her hair in schoolgirl piglets or wear cute hair slides (barrettes) and suck on a lollipop.

SCENE 28 WHO'S THE BOSS?

Basic Plot
**He has an important assignment for her
– to pleasure him.**

Getting It On Game for Newbies

He's behind the desk, talking on the phone.
She's the temp, working in the other room, on
the computer. He sends her an email saying
he needs her assistance right away. When
she comes in, she finds that he's unzipped his
trousers and has an erection. He tells her she
has a five-minute deadline to bring him off.

Getting It On Game for Experienced Scenesters

She hides underneath the boss's big desk before an
"important meeting". Slowly – and very quietly – she
performs oral sex on him with the clients sitting right there.
His challenge? To keep a straight face and continue with his
meeting. Alternatively, he may be on the phone and has to
continue with his phone conversation without faltering.

Getting It On Game for
Hardcore Role-Players

Take the above action to his
actual place of work.

Dress It Up

For Him:
* Suit
* Shirt
* Tie

For Her:
* Prim skirt
* Blouse
* Sensible shoes
* Tights

XXX Rating
He gives you very suggestive dictation.

Make It Real
Threaten to bring him up on sexual harassment charges – that is, if he doesn't give you a pay rise!

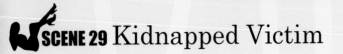

SCENE 29 Kidnapped Victim

Basic Plot
She's a wealthy bluest-of-blood duchess
abducted by a rakish highwayman who
demands sex instead of money as ransom.

Getting It On Game for Newbies
She is taking some air out in the garden and doesn't see
him coming. He sneaks up behind and slips a blindfold
over her eyes and, using a scarf/rope/handcuffs, ties her
arms behind her back. He says that she is now under his
control and marches her into the bedroom. He unties her.
Whispering dirty words in her ear, he begins to seduce
her, running his hands up and down her clothed body,
undressing her hurriedly. You finish with wild sex.

Getting It On Game for Experienced Scenesters
He reties her hands so they are now
above her head/attached to the bedposts.
He keeps the restraints on and tears
her clothing off. He then proceeds to
tease and torment her body until she is
straining against her bonds and begging
him to take her now.

Getting It On Game for Hardcore Role-Players

As he brings her to the bedroom, she struggles and tells him she will never succumb, no matter what he does to her. He ties her bottom up on the bed and proceeds to lightly spank her. He asks if she will be a good girl. She meekly promises to do anything he wants as long as he doesn't hurt her.

Dress It Up

For Him:
* White shirt open to navel
* Some sort of fake weapon
* High boots
* Three-day beard

For Her:
Long gown with lots of buttons

XXX Rating
Keep the blindfold on.

Make It Real
She should try and speak in an uppercust accent, while he can use more common language. In the end, as in all the best historical romances, she should fall in love with him.

SCENE 30 AT YOUR COMMAND

Basic Plot

Your lover is your love slave, at your sexual beck and call.

 Getting It On Game for Newbies

The Master starts by ordering the Slave to do small tasks – getting them a drink, fluffing pillows, giving a foot massage. They should order, not ask, and keep an expressionless face. They don't have to worry about the "no, you first honey" niceties of sex; this all about their pleasure, and their pleasure alone. The Master then announces to the Slave that they are now free… to service them.

Getting It On Game for Experienced Scenesters

The Master should tell their Slave exactly and explicitly what they are going to do to them or want them to do. This gives the Slave a chance to object… and also to anticipate –"I'm going to tie your hands up high and then I'm going to spank you with my hand until your bottom turns pink. Then I'm going to tickle you all over with feathers while you are helpless" or "I'm going to spread my legs and I want you to use your tongue on me until I say stop." Do not say, "Are you okay?", "Did I hurt you?", "Are you sure you're enjoying this?"

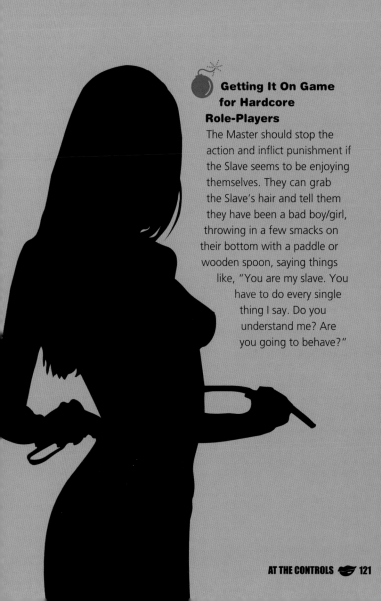

Getting It On Game for Hardcore Role-Players

The Master should stop the action and inflict punishment if the Slave seems to be enjoying themselves. They can grab the Slave's hair and tell them they have been a bad boy/girl, throwing in a few smacks on their bottom with a paddle or wooden spoon, saying things like, "You are my slave. You have to do every single thing I say. Do you understand me? Are you going to behave?"

Dress It Up

For Him:

As slave:
* Black briefs, preferably leather and skimpy

As Master, add:
* A leather jacket
* Black trousers
* Stockings and a push-up bra
* Knee-high or thigh-high boots
* A blindfold, scarves or old stockings to tie him up
* A wooden spoon or hairbrush

For Her:

As Slave:
* A black, preferably leather, bustier
* Black thong

As Master, add:
* Black silk lingerie
* High black boots

XXX Rating
This is an ideal role to suggest things you wouldn't dare during "normal" lovemaking.

Make It Real
Call each other Master and Slave rather than by name.

SCENE 31 NO! NO! **OH YES! YESSSSSS!**

Basic Plot
In this favourite female fantasy,
he takes her against her will.

 ## Getting It On Game for Newbies

She is alone in her bedroom, naked. He sneaks
up behind her, covers her eyes and mouth and
says, "I won't hurt you if you do everything I
say." She's helpless as he takes his hand from
her eyes and explores and strokes her body. He
challenges her to tell him she is not enjoying
what he is doing. Sigh. She can't.

Getting It On Game for Experienced Scenesters

Coming to her senses, she tries to escape. They wrestle. He grabs
her by the hair, pulls her arms behind her back, and forces her head
down to his crotch. He unzips and orders her to take care of him.

 ## Getting It On Game for Hardcore Role-Players

After she has reluctantly whipped
him into a frenzy, he pins her
down, thrusting her thighs apart
with his knee and penetrates her
as savagely as he can.

Dress It Up

For Him:
* Street clothes

For Her:
* Birthday suit

XXX Rating
Because this involves a lot of unbridled force, before you start set up a code word to stop the action if it gets too much.

Make It Real

She wants to feel completely overpowered so he should be as forceful as he can without actually hurting her – running his fingers through her hair and pulling, nibbling roughly at her skin, ripping her clothes without care.

INDEX AND WEBSITES

Adult film listings:

Game Link
www.gamelink.com

Film scripts for reading and downloading:

Internet Movie Script Database
www.imsdb.com

Simply Scripts
www.simplyscripts.com

Virtual games:

Playskins
www.playskins.com

Second Life
www.secondlife.com

The Sims
www.thesims2.ea.com

Sociolotron SM
www.sociolotron.amerabyte.com

Sex toys and fancy dress costumes:

Ann Summers
www.annsummers.com

Babeland
www.babeland.com

Coco de Mer
www.coco-de-mer.com

Love Honey
www.lovehoney.co.uk

Ooh La La
www.ooh-lala.co.uk

Party Domain
www.partydomain.co.uk

The Pleasure Chest
www.thepleasurechest.com

Simply Pleasure
www.simplypleasure.com

Temptations
www.temptationsdirect.co.uk

Tabooboo
www.tabooboo.com